Antique Colours for Primitive Rugs

Formulas Using Cushing's Acid Dyes

by

Emma Lou Lais

and

Barbara Carroll

ERRATA
Please note
these changes:
p. 27 #6 - Nicholas Red -
2t Terra Cotta
Colour Wheel page -
Browns and **Neutrals**

Published by
W. Cushing & Company
Kennebunkport, Maine USA

Cover rug "Pumpkin Vines"
Designed by Emma Lou Lais
Hooked by Barbara Carroll
Cover photo by Wayne Carroll

ISBN 9-9651811-0-3

Manufactured in the United States of America
Published March 29, 1996
First Printing

Contents

Emma Lou and Barb

wish to thank

Wayne Carroll
Pat Lais
Dolly Shumber
Robin Carroll
Pat Moshimer
Paul Moshimer

for all their help, support and enthusiasm.

They warmed our hearts.

FORWORD

Barbara and I met over the telephone. Its funny how you can get to know someone that way, without ever actually meeting them face to face. Anyway, Barbara told me one day last year that she and Emma Lou wanted to write a dyeing book for primitives using our new acid dyes. I immediately told her that we would help in any way we could. And so began a great adventure.

In October, 1995, we agreed to met at Barbara's house in Ligonier, Penn. in mid-January. What were we thinking!? This winter turned out to be one of the hardest winters on record for the Northeast, but we caught a bit of January thaw between a blizzard and a flood. The meeting went off without a hitch.

When I first walked in to Barbara's sunny studio, I was dazzled by what I saw. Now I've literally grown up around rug hooking and colour, but the swatches that these two great gals had laid out before me were a feast for the eyes. The richness and depth they have achieved using our acid dyes is so satisfying to me personally, after having struggled for the last two years to basically reinvent these 94 acid dye formulas. This convinced me that we are on the right track.

We wanted his book to be a departure from the other dye formula books. We wanted to actually show these swatches in colour in the book so that the reader could see what they were going to get with each formula and to see what is possible using these new acid dyes.

I hope you enjoy this process, so like the old time dyers say, " Put the tea kettle on and let's do some dyein'."

Paul Moshimer
Kennebunkport, Maine
March 1996

A BIT ABOUT US

Emma Lou Lais:

Emma Lou has been a primitive rug hooking teacher and designer for the past 15 years. She began hooking in 1939 having been taught by her mother. She studied with the late Margaret Hunt Masters.

Her design and colour sense have made her one of the favorites in the primitive rug hooking field.

Emma Lou's catalogue of designs (a true delight) is available directly from her.

Emma Lou teaches primitive rug hooking at Woolley Fox Primitive Workshop, Ligonier, Pennsylvania, and Green Mountain Rug School, Randolph Center, Vermont. She is also available for other workshops in Kansas City and around the country.

Emma Lou and her English Springer Spaniel, Molly, reside in Kansas City, Missouri.

Barbara Carroll:

Barb has been teaching primitive rug hooking for five years. She started hooking in 1987, as a student of Emma Lou's.

She is known for her use of textured wools, colour eye and sense of whimsy. Her stash of textured wools is legendary.

In May, Barb hosts the annual Woolley Fox Primitive Workshop in Ligonier, Pennsylvania. She and her husband, Wayne, also own the Woolley Fox Bed & Breakfast (ask her and she'll tell you how Woolley Fox got it's name).

Barb also teaches primitive workshops at the Woolley Fox.

A BIT ABOUT US continued

She has written several articles for *Rug Hooking* Magazine, including a "teacher feature" about Emma Lou, and articles on recycled wools and how to use textured wools in primitive rugs.

Emma Lou and Barb have worked hard separately and together to develop these soft, rich antique colours so desired by primitive rug hookers. They are both available separately and together (more fun) for dye workshops. To schedule a great fun, learning time, contact either one at:

Emma Lou Lais
8643 Hiawatha Road
Kansas City, MO 64114
Phone: 816-444-1777

Barbara Carroll
61 Lincoln Hwy., East
Ligonier, PA 15658
Phone: 412-238-3004

GET YOUR STUFF TOGETHER

Your dye equipment must always be kept totally separate from your kitchen equipment. Never, never use your dye equipment in your food preparation; and, if possible, a totally separate dye area is the best. It's not wonderful for our darlings to come home and reach for a spoon to taste that interesting-looking chili when what's in the pot is wool in *Old Maine Red*!!

We recommend the following equipment:

Plenty of white enamel pots (no nicks or rust spots in them). You can find them at flea markets or antique shops, and they are also available at K-Marts. White pots enable you to see what colour the dye is and how much has been absorbed into the wool. Don't use anything else.

Measuring spoons and TOD spoons. The TOD spoons are available from Cushing and are wonderful for the smaller measures.

Rubber gloves. We use two weights of gloves. The regular weight for measuring and mixing the dyes, and Bluettes, which are heavy and wonderful for handling the wool when it is so hot. The Bluettes are available at hardware stores.

Scissors to cut wool.

Kitchen whisks to stir dry dye and boiling water in measuring cup.

White paper towels for checking dye color in dye bath.

Wooden spoons for stirring wool in pot.

Pot holders.

Salt – uniodized.

STUFF continued

White vinegar.

Clorox Bleach (to clean pots after dyeing).

Ivory Liquid.

Apron.

Glass jars for storing leftover liquid dyes; labels for jars and lids.

Glass measuring cups.

Good quality wools.

Cushing Colour Chart. The Colour Chart is important. It allows you to see exactly which colours you are working with; and, if you have to substitute you will be able to see which is the closest colour.

And, most important, Cushing Acid Dyes.

LET'S GET STARTED

Now we begin a truly exciting adventure into the world of colour, and sometimes a scary place (isn't the unknown just a smidgen nerve-wracking??).

We never do "short cuts." Dyeing the wool is truly one of the most important parts of achieving a great rug. So, take extra time and you will "hug" your results.

We both soak our wools in warm water (enough to cover the wool) and a few drops of Ivory Liquid soap (don't get the water too soapy) overnight. Emma Lou soaks in the washer and Barb in a big white enamel bath tub. We both use good quality wools. Remember, you are creating heirlooms so always put into the rug the best that is available to you.

First, put on your rubber gloves. Always, always use rubber gloves when you are handling the dyes - wet or dry.

Next, mix the dyes according to the dye formula. Some formulas require mixing all dry dyes in boiling water together, and others require mixing each dye separately in boiling water. So, read each dye formula carefully and follow the directions.

Open the dye envelope and take out the plastic package (yes, it's a pain to use). Hold the edge of the plastic package and shake the contents. Clip off the top or corner of the package, then put in your measuring spoon and STIR the dry dye. Remember, Cushing dyes are blended (which gives us our wonderful colours) and, by stirring the dry dye, you will redistribute it correctly. When measuring dry dye into measuring spoon, don't pack, just level softly.

Then measure the dry dye according to your formula directions into a glass measuring cup and carefully pour in the amount of BOILING

GETTING STARTED continued

water the formula calls for. The water must be boiling to dissolve the dyes. Then use your whisk to stir it all up.

THE FORMULAS

There are two methods of mixing the formulas in this book. We call them the *A LA CARTE METHOD* and the *POT LUCK METHOD*. Each formula is labeled with the method used. Let's do a walk through, of each of the methods.

A LA CARTE METHOD

Using the *A LA CARTE METHOD* , you mix each dry dye individually in boiling water, and then add a specified amount of the liquid dye solution to the dye pot.

For instance, using the **#1A - JESSIES'S RED APPLE** formula, you would proceed as follows:

1. Dissolve 1/2 teaspoon Egyptian Red dye into 1 cup of boiling water in a glass measuring cup and set aside.

2. Dissolve 1/2 teaspoon Reseda Green dye into 1 cup of boiling water in a glass measuring cup and set aside.

3. Dissolve 1/2 teaspoon Medium Brown dye into 1 cup of boiling water in a glass measuring cup and set aside.

4. Prepare the dye pot with water and salt, then add the specified amounts of each dye solution, in this case
   1 cup Egyptian Red dye solution
   4 tablespoons Reseda Green dye solution
   2 tablespoons Medium Brown dye solution

5. Then proceed following the dyeing directions.

Be sure to read the *A LA CARTE METHOD*

GETTING STARTED continued

formulas carefully; they do not all use 1/2 teaspoon of dry dye to 1 cup of boiling water. Note that formula #91 – Antique Brown–Black is one that uses different amounts of dry dye to different amounts of boiling water

This is not a complicated method; just another way to create these great antique colours.

THE POT LUCK METHOD

Using the *POT LUCK METHOD*, you add all of the specified dry dyes in a glass measuring cup, and then add the specified amount of boiling water.

For instance, using the **#72 – BARB'S MAGIC SHOW** formula, you would proceed as follows:

1. Measure the following amounts of these dry dyes into a glass measuring cup:
   3/4 teaspoon Turquoise
   3/8 teaspoon Jade Green
   1/4 teaspoon & 2/32 teaspoon Br. Purple
   3/32 teaspoon Garnet
   1/4 teaspoon Chartreuse

2. Add one cup of boiling water to these dry dyes, whisk, dissolving completely.

3. Prepare the dye pot with water and salt, then add the specified amount of the dye solution, which , using this formula, is:
1/4 cup + 1/8 cup (3/8 cup) dye solution

4. Then proceed following the dyeing directions.

Be sure to read the *POT LUCK METHOD* formulas carefully so that you are using the required amounts of dry dyes to the required amounts of boiling water.

DYEING DIRECTIONS

Now off to the stove. Fill your pots about 2/3 full with water. Add the required amount of dye and SALT (we know Paul, your chemist, doesn't agree). Use 1 tablespoon of uniodized salt per pot. The salt helps to distribute the dye particles and provides more even dyed colours (no weird spot surprises). Bring the pot almost to a boil, add your wool, use 1/2 yard per pot for all of these formulas, turn heat down to medium or medium-low, stir a few times during the next 20-35 minutes, and then add your white vinegar. We "glug" it – but use about 1/3 cup. Stir again and simmer another 15 to 20 minutes. The water should clear. If it doesn't, just simmer a little longer, adding 1/4 cup more vinegar.

Some colours take longer to absorb into the wool, especially if you are working with the deep colours.

After the water has cleared, take the pot off the stove and remove the wool <u>carefully</u> to avoid being scalded.

Now to rinse the wools:

Emma Lou rinses immediately, starting with hot water and reducing heat of water temperature until she is using lukewarm water.

Barb lets the wool cool down to room temperature in the sink and then rinses in the washing machine. She uses the wash cycle (no soap) for about 4 minutes and then lets it finish the rinse/spin cycle.

But, whatever method, make sure you rinse the wool thoroughly and <u>don't</u> cool too fast – you will felt the wool and have to learn to make Penny Rugs!!

Dry the wool in the dryer using medium heat

DYEING DIRECTIONS continued

with a big fluffy towel. Then remove your beautiful new colours and smile, smile, smile!

If you are dyeing quite a bit and will be reusing your pot immediately, empty it and begin the dye process again. Use fresh water, add the salt and the new dyes. Don't ever use the same water twice. It contains vinegar and the wool will absorb the dye before you are ready.

When you are finished dyeing for the day, clean dye pots by rinsing out with water, then fill them with water and bleach and let them sit until sparkling white again. Rinse with water and a little Ivory Liquid, dry and put away.

Store any leftover liquid dyes in glass jars. Be sure to mark the colours on both the jar and the lid. When reusing these dyes, stir well and, after you add them to the dye pot, make sure that the water, dye and salt are almost at a boil. You can also heat the dyes in the glass jar in a pan of hot water to make sure the dye is once again fully dissolved.

DYEING OVER TEXTURED WOOL

We both use lots and lots of textured wools in our teaching and hooking.

Dyeing over the textured wool is so exciting. The results just fill your heart with a wonderful happiness. Don't be afraid to experiment. What's the worst than can happen – a colour, not exactly what you expected, but can be used in a future rug, and then a chance to try again. Often times, the "mistakes" are great surprises!

We rarely (Barb never) dye over white wool. As you read our formulas, you will see we use lots of different colours of textured wools; and, of course, many times the plaids or

DYEING DIRECTIONS continued

checks will have numerous colours to them, so your dyed wools will then have lots of different tones. Big fun to work with, and will add greatly to the antique look of your rug.

Another bit of fun... you want greens, and are planning on using the Olive Green and Bronze Green mix... yes, you dye this over tans, camels, taupes, light and medium brown wools. So now throw in some pink, lavender, yellow and aqua wools and you will come up with many different colours of green, but with all the same tone to them. Sort of like our kids!

We dye over just about all manner of wools; plaids, checks, heathers, tweeds, herringbones, and solids. We both prefer 100% wool, but will use 80% wool/20% other if that is what is available and we love the wool.

One of the most asked questions we get is, "What would you dye over this?" So we offer this guide:

Tan, taupe, camel, medium brown wools – over dye with reds, greens, browns, golds.

Green wools – reds, and greens and antique black-green.

Gray wools – blues, blue-reds, blue-greens and greens, antique black-brown, touch of black, Old Gold for a great mustard.

Red wools – antique black.

Blue wools – blue, blue-greens, antique black.

Turquoise wool – terra-cotta dye.

Hot pink wool – green dyes.

Purple wool – mulberry or maroon dye.

DYEING DIRECTIONS continued

One of the ways we achieve different shades of the same colour is to use various wools in the same colour family in the dye pot. For instances, beiges, camels and medium browns, and then over-dye them with **#6 - Nicholas Red**. Don't forget – just for fun, throw in some green or rust wools. Again, the same colour family, just different tones.

Always keep in mind that adding unusual colours can add a lot to your Primitive Rugs... sort of a spark or poison.

Sometimes we need the old, faded colours for barns, houses, flowers, leaves, trees, pasture animals, etc. So, use a lesser amount of the dye formula - over heathery wools. Your choice of wools is very important. They must be light, grayed-off, subtle wools. They may be various colours of wools. We suggest taupe, grays, beiges, greens, in this order.

With this book, Cushing Dyes and good wools your rugs will have a wonderful sense of colour and a great antique look.

Okay, you want to dye and don't have all the dyes for the formula you want. Look at your Cushing Colour Chart and see which dye you have that's closest to the one you are missing, then simply experiment. One of the most wonderful things about these antique colours and Primitive Rugs is we don't have to match exactly. This is a great sense of freedom for our rug hooking and, again, often times produces a better Primitive Rug. So just go for it!

THE NEW CUSHING'S ACID DYES

A word about the new Cushing Acid Dyes and the "formulas" using the old Union Dyes. You will <u>not</u> get the same results; but, using our formulas, your colour eye, the colour wheel and the Cushing Colour Chart will enable you to come close to what you want. If the red you are working with needs to be more blue-red, add a little blue. Or, if the "blue" formula tends toward the purple, go to the colour wheel, find the compliment (Old Gold, Nugget Gold, Buttercup Yellow, etc.), add a little and that will bring you close to what you are trying to achieve.

These dyes are good, and we will and are getting wonderful colours using them. In life there is always change and adjustment, so march straight forward, pick up your dye pot and spoon and begin a great new world of colour with these dyes.

<u>Remember</u>, you cannot hurry these new dyes. Let them simmer and develop at their own speed. And don't be nervous about the colour of wools in the dye pot. As they simmer and the wools absorb <u>all</u> the dye, your colour will be right.

For instance, using formula **#34 - Saturday Surprise**, the Khaki Drab dye absorbs into the wool before the Medium Brown dye. So, most important, be patient... and follow the directions.

The formulas in this book have many backgrounds. Some have been developed by Emma Lou, some by Barb, and some by both of us. Others have been given to us by friends or "Rug School" acquaintances. And, to all of you, a big thanks!

These formulas have all been dyed and tested with Cushing Acid Dyes. We do not guarantee that you will achieve the same results if you are using the old Union dyes.

THE NEW CUSHING'S ACID DYES cont.

Also, keep in mind that the water in your area may be different from ours, causing your colours to be somewhat different.

If you have well water and are not happy with your results, we suggest trying bottled water.

We want you to have fun with this book and the Cushing Acid Dyes. Remember, Primitive Rug Hooking is <u>not</u> an exact science – it's a casual fun use of antique colours, wonderful wools and designs, and a great imagination!

As you dye these formulas (and won't you have fun?!), keep samples of what you dye and eventually you will have a wonderful set of swatches.

WHILE WE DYED EVERYTHING OVER WHITE TO "KEY" THE COLOURS FOR THIS BOOK – WE REALLY RECOMMEND WOOLS OTHER THAN WHITE.

LIST OF CUSHING ACID DYES USED IN THESE FORMULAS

We have compiled the following list of dyes showing the tally of how many times they appear in the formulas to assist in keeping an inventory.

American Beauty	4
Apricot	1
Aqua	1
Black	16
Blue	8
Bright Purple	6
Bronze	10
Bronze Green	11
Burgundy	2
Buttercup Yellow	6
Canary	1
Cardinal	1
Champagne	2
Chartreuse	8
Copenhagen Blue	3
Dark Brown	5
Dark Gray	3
Dark Green	6
Ecru	3
Egyptian Red	6
Garnet	4
Gold	7
Golden Brown	11
Hunter Green	4
Jade Green	5
Khaki	1
Khaki Drab	18
Mahogany	11
Maroon	4
Medium Brown	20
Mulberry	3
Mummy Brown	2
Myrtle Green	1
Navy Blue	1
Nugget Gold	5
Old Gold	7
Old Ivory	1
Old Rose	1
Olive Green	11
Orange	2
Peacock	3
Plum	6
Reseda Green	3
Rust	10
Seal Brown	5
Silver Gray	6
Sky Blue	1
Spice Brown	3
Taupe	3
Terra Cotta	7
Turkey Red	3
Turquoise	3
Turquoise Blue	2
Turquoise Green	1
Wild Rose	1
Wine	1
Wood Rose	5
Yellow	1

The Formulas for

REDS

&

PURPLES

#1A – JESSIE'S RED APPLE
A LA CARTE METHOD

Mix:

1/2 t	Egyptian Red – 1 CBW
1/2 t	Reseda Green – 1 CBW
1/2 t	Medium Brown – 1 CBW

Use in pot:

1 cup	Egyptian Red
1 T	Reseda Green
2 T	Medium Brown

Wools: camel and beige.

#1B – NANCY'S NAUGHTY RED
A LA CARTE METHOD

Mix:

1/2 t	Egyptian Red – 1 CBW
1/2 t	American Beauty – 1 CBW
1/2 t	Reseda Green – 1 CBW
1/2 t	Medium Brown – 1 CBW

Use in pot:

1/2 cup	Egyptian Red
1/2 cup	American Beauty
2 T	Reseda Green
1 T	Medium Brown

For lighter shades use in pot:

2 T	Egyptian Red
2 T	American Beauty
1-1/2 t	Reseda Green
1/2 t	Medium Brown

Wools: camel and beige.

#2A – OLD MAINE
POT LUCK METHOD

1/2 t	Turkey Red	⎫
1/4 t	Mahogany	⎬ 1 CBW
1/2 t	Medium Brown	⎮
1/2 t	Khaki Drab	⎭

Lighter – 1/4 cup dye solution
Medium – 1/2 cup dye solution
Darker – 3/4 cup dye solution

Wools: beige, camel, medium grayed green.

#2B – SHAKESPEARE RED
POT LUCK METHOD

3/4 t	Turkey Red	⎫
1/4 t	Mahogany	⎬ 1 CBW
1/4 t	Khaki Drab	⎭

Lighter –1/4 cup dye solution
Darker – 1/2 cup dye solution

Wools: beige, camel, medium grayed green.

#4 – GARNET
A LA CARTE METHOD

Mix:
1/2 t   Garnet – 1 CBW
1/2 t   Bronze Green – 1 CBW

Use in pot:
3/4 cup Garnet
4 1/2 t Gronze Green

Wools: camel, tan, green, red and beige plaid

#5 – TACO BEAN RED
POT LUCK METHOD

3/4 t	Mahogany	
1/2 t	Mulberry	} 1 CBW
1/4 t+2/32 t	Terra Cotta	

Lighter – 1/4 cup dye solution
Darker – 1/2 cup dye solution

Wools: camel, tan, beige, green plaid.

#6 – NICHOLAS RED
POT LUCK METHOD

2 T	Terra Cotta	
1/2 t	American Beauty	} 1 CBW
1/8 t	Mahogany	
1 t	Buttercup Yellow	

Lighter – 1/4 cup dye solution
Darker – 1/2 cup dye solution

Wools: camel, tan, beige and green plaid.

#8 – BUTTERMILK PAINT RED
A LA CARTE METHOD

Mix:
1/2 t   Terra Cotta – 1 CBW
1/2 t   Khaki Drab – 1 CBW

Use in pot:
1 cup   Terra Cotta and
4 T   Khaki Drab

Wools: camel, cream, green plaid, beige, red, and tan.

#9 - ASHES OF ROSE
POT LUCK METHOD

1/2 t	Egyptian Red	⎫
1/16 t	Khaki Drab	⎬ 1 CBW
1/32 t	Blue	⎭

Lighter – 1/3 cup dye solution
Darker – 2/3 cup dye solution

Wools: camel and lots of funky, different tan-beige plaid.

#10 - BOBBIE'S TERRIFIC TERRA COTTA
POT LUCK METHOD

1/2 t	Terra Cotta	⎫
1/4 t	Dark Brown	⎬ 1 CBW
1/16 t	Bronze Green	⎭

Lighter – 1/4 cup dye solution
Darker – 1/2 cup dye solution

Wools: tan, camel.

#12 - EMMA LOU'S FAVORITE RED
POT LUCK METHOD

3/8 t	Buttercup Yellow	⎫
3 t	Terra Cotta	⎬ 1 CBW
1/2 t	American Beauty	⎭

Lighter – 1/3 cup dye solution
Darker – 2/3 cup dye solution

Wools: camel plaids and checks, tan, green and red plaids.
Great background if using 1 cup of formula.

#13 – HOOKED ON REDS
POT LUCK METHOD

2 t	Maroon	⎫
1 1/2 t	Mahogany	⎬ 1 CBW
1/2 t	Black	⎭

Use all

Wools: browns, beiges, camels, tans.

#14 – DEEP PURPLE
POT LUCK METHOD

1 3/4 t	Bright Purple	⎫
1/4 t	Chartreuse	⎬ 1 CBW
		⎭

Use all.

Wools: grays and brown plaids.
Great dark background.

#15 – MOLLY'S PURPLE GARNET
POT LUCK METHOD

3/4 t	Bright Purple	⎫
1/2 t	Garnet	⎬ 1 CBW
2/32 t	Chartreuse	⎭

Use 1/4 cup.

Wools: grays, beige-taupe plaid.

#16 – MULBERRY PATCH
POT LUCK METHOD

3/4 t	Bright Purple	⎫
1/2 t	Mulberry	⎬ 1 CBW
2/32 t	Chartreuse	⎭

Use 1/4 cup.

Wools: grays, beige-taupe plaid.

The Formulas for

GREENS

#20 - EVERGREEN
A LA CARTE METHOD

Mix:
1/2 t	Olive Green	- 1 CBW
1/2 t	Hunter Green	- 1 CBW

In pot use:
6 T	Olive Green
3 T	Hunter Green

Wools: medium and dark grays.

#21 - BARB'S RESEDA
A LA CARTE METHOD

Mix:
1/2 t	Reseda Green	- 1 CBW
1/2 t	Olive Green	- 1 CBW
1/2 t	Black	- 1 CBW

In pot use:
6 T	Reseda Green
1 1/2 T	Olive Green
1 1/2 T	Black

Wools: medium to dark grays.
NOTE: Simmer a long time.

#22 - OUR OLD RESEDA
A LA CARTE METHOD

Mix:
1/2 t	Dark Green	- 1 CBW
1/2 t	Silver Gray	- 1 CBW
1/2 t	Bronze Green	- 1 CBW

In pot use:
3 T	Dark Green
3 T	Silver Gray
9 T	Bronze Green

Wools: beiges with greens - grays.

#23 - JUNIPER BLUE-GREEN
A LA CARTE METHOD

Mix:
1/2 t	Silver Gray	– 1 CBW
1/2 t	Dark Green	– 1 CBW
1 1/2 t	Olive Green	– 1 CBW
1 1/2 t	Black	– 1 CBW

In pot use:
3 T	Silver Gray
3 T	Dark Green
1 1/2 T	Olive Green
1 1/2 T	Black

Wools: grayed greens and grays.

#24 - BARB'S MARVELOUS MYRTLE
A LA CARTE METHOD

Mix:
1/2 t	Myrtle Green	– 1 CBW
1/2 t	Mahogany	– 1 CBW
1/2 t	Black	– 1 CBW
1/2 t	Dark Green	– 1 CBW

In pot use:
1/2 cup	Myrtle Green
1 T+1 t	Mahogany
1 T	Black
1/2 cup	Dark Green

Wools: grays. Deep tones great for background.

#25 - BRONZE/GREEN
POT LUCK METHOD

1 t	Bronze Green	⎫
3/8 t	Golden Brown	⎬ 1 CBW
1/2 t	Chartreuse	⎭

Use 1/4 cup.

Wools: beiges – plaids with beige and red and green and camel.

#26 – BRONZE/GREEN
POT LUCK METHOD

1 t	Bronze Green	⎫
3/8 t	Medium Brown	⎬ 1 CBW
1/2 t	Nugget Gold	⎭

Use 1/4 cup.

Wools: beige, camel, plaids with beige, red and green.

#27 – OLIVE GREEN/PLUM
POT LUCK METHOD

1 t	Olive Green	⎫
4/32 t	Chartreuse	⎬ 1 CBW
2/32 t	Plum	⎭

Use 1/4 cup.

Wools: beige, camel, plaids with beige, red and green.

#28 – OLIVE & BRONZE GREEN
A LA CARTE METHOD

Mix:
1/2 t	Olive Green – 1 CBW
1/2 t	Bronze Green – 1 CBW

In pot mix:
3 T	Olive Green
3 T	Bronze Green

Could do:
2 T	Olive Green
4 T	Bronze Green
	(Just to mix them all up.)

Mix: The mix can be equal – Olive Green & Bronze Green – or more Bronze Green and less Olive Green – or more Olive Green and less Bronze Green – add as much dye as you would to get either lighter or darker shades.

Wools: beige, camels, plaids with beige, red and green.

#29 - KHAKI/BRONZE
POT LUCK METHOD

1 t	Khaki	⎱
1 t	Bronze	⎰ 1 CBW

Lighter - 1/4 cup dye solution
Darker - 3/4 cup dye solution

Wools: beige, camels, plaids with beige, red and green.

#30 - KHAKI DRAB
A LA CARTE METHOD

1/2 t   Khaki Drab - 1 CBW
Use 1/2 cup.

Wools: beige, camels, plaids with beige, red and green. A great dye to be used as is over the above wools for a great old look in our primitive rugs.

#31- MYSTERIOUS GREEN
POT LUCK METHOD

1/4 t	Bronze Green	
1/4 t	Olive Green	
1/4 t	Hunter Green	1 CBW
3/32 t	Plum	
1/32 t	Chartreuse	

Use 1/4 to 1/2 cup.

Wools: beige, camels, plaids with beige, red and green.

#32 - EMMA LOU'S HUNTER
A LA CARTE METHOD

Mix:
1/2 t   Hunter Green - 1 CBW
1/2 t   Olive Green - 1 CBW

In pot use:
5 T   Hunter Green
4 T   Olive Green

Wools: grays.

#33 – GERRY'S MOON AND STAR
POT LUCK METHOD

1/2 t	Khaki Drab	⎫
1/16 t	Olive Green	⎬ 1 CBW
1/16 t	Turkey Red	⎭

Use 1/2 cup.

Wools: beige, camels, plaids with beige, red and green.

#34 – SATURDAY SURPRISE
A LA CARTE METHOD

1 t   Khaki Drab – 2 CBW
1/2 t   Medium Brown – 1 CBW

For light use:
8 T   Khaki Drab
1 T   Medium Brown

For mediums:
10 T   Khaki Drab
1 1/2 T   Medium Brown

For darks:
14 T   Khaki Drab
2 T   Medium Brown

Wools: beiges, tans, camels, plaids, and herringbone textures.

The Formulas for

GOLDS

#40A – NEW YORK BRONZE
POT LUCK METHOD

1 t	Bronze	⎫	
3/8 t	Medium Brown	⎬	1 CBW
1/2 t	Nugget Gold	⎭	

Use 1/4 cup.

Wools: beige, tan, gray.

#40B – BRONZY SPARK
POT LUCK METHOD

1/32 t	Golden Brown	⎫	
1/8 t	Bronze	⎬	1 CBW
1/16 t	Gold	⎭	

Use **3/4 cup**.

Wools: beige, tan, gray.

#40C – KANSAS CITY BRONZE
POT LUCK METHOD

1/2 t	Bronze	⎫	
3/8 t	Medium Brown	⎬	1 CBW
1 t	Nugget Gold	⎭	

Use 1/4 cup.

Wools: beige, tan, gray.

#41 – BIG AL GOLD
POT LUCK METHOD

3/4 t	Golden Brown	⎫
1 t	Gold	⎬ 1 CBW
2/32 t	Spice Brown	⎭

Use 1/4 cup.

Wools: beige, tan, gray.

#42 – OUR NEW GOLDEN BROWN
POT LUCK METHOD

1/2 t	Nugget Gold	⎫
1/4 t	Medium Brown	⎬ 1 CBW
		⎭

Use 1/2 cup.

Wools: beige, tan, gray.

Mix & <u>keep dry</u> for use in 45A, 45B, 46 & 47
1/2 t   Nugget Gold
1/4 t   Medium Brown

#43 – BARB'S GREAT GOLD
POT LUCK METHOD

3/4 t	Old Gold	⎫
1/4 t	Gold	⎬ 1 CBW
1 t	Champagne	⎭

For more mellow as shown use 1/4 cup.

1/2 t	Old Gold	⎫
1/2 t	Gold	⎬ 1 CBW
3/4 t	Champagne	⎭

For brighter – swatch not shown.

Wools: beige; gray makes great mustard.

#44 – BARB'S NIFTY NUGGET
A LA CARTE METHOD

Mix:

1/2 t	Nugget Gold – 1 CBW
1/2 t	Bronze – 1 CBW
1/2 t	Medium Brown – 1 CBW

In pot use:

8 T	Nugget Gold
1 T	Bronze
2 T	Medium Brown

Wools: beige, gray, etc.

#45A – ANTIQUE GOLD
POT LUCK METHOD

1/2 t	Khaki Drab	⎫
1/16 t	New Golden Brown*	⎬ 1 CBW
1/16 t	Woodrose	⎮
1/32 t	Old Gold	⎭

Use 1/4 cup.

Wools: beige, tan, gray. Darker shades great background.

#45B – ANTIQUE GOLD
POT LUCK METHOD

1/2 t	New Golden Brown*	⎫
1/16 t	Khaki Drab	⎬ 1 CBW
1/16 t	Woodrose	⎮
1/32 t	Old Gold	⎭

Use 1/4 cup.

Wools: beige, tan, gray.

*see note after #42

#46 – OLDE GOLD
POT LUCK METHOD

3/4 t	New Golden Brown*	
1 t	Buttercup Yellow	} 1 CBW
1/16 t	Yellow	

We used 1/4 cup - you could use less.

Wools: beige, tan, gray.

#47 – CALIFORNIA GOLD
POT LUCK METHOD

1 t	New Golden Brown*	
3/4 t	Gold	} 1 CBW

Light – 1/8 cup dye solution
Medium – 1/4 cup dye solution

Wools: beige, tan, gray.

#48 – NEAT GOLD
POT LUCK METHOD

1/2 t	Old Gold	
1/4 t	Canary	} 1 CBW
1/16 t	Seal Brown	

Use all of the dye.

Wools: beige, tan, gray.

#49 – MUSTARD
POT LUCK METHOD

1/2 t	Old Gold	
1/4 t	Buttercup Yellow	} 1 CBW

Use 1/4 cup.

Wools: grays.

*see note after #42

#50 – BRICK GOLD
POT LUCK METHOD

1/4 t	Buttercup Yellow	⎫	
1/2 t	Old Gold	⎬	1 CBW
1/8	Bronze	⎭	

Use 1 cup.

Wools: grays.

#51 – VERMONT GOLD
POT LUCK METHOD

1/8 t	Buttercup Yellow	⎫	
1/2 t	Old Gold	⎬	1 CBW
1/4 t	Bronze	⎭	

Use 1/2 cup.

Wools: grays.

#52 – NUTMEG
POT LUCK METHOD

1 t	Golden Brown	⎫	
3/4 t	Gold	⎬	1 CBW
1/32 t	Spice Brown	⎪	
2/32 t	Dark Gray	⎭	

Use 1/4 cup.

Wools: tan, light beige, medium beige.

The Formulas for

BLUES

#60 - JO'S SMOKY BLUE
A LA CARTE METHOD

Mix:
1/2 t   Silver Gray - 1 CBW
1/2 t   Blue - 1 CBW

Use:
2 T+2 t Silver Gray
1 T+1 t Blue

Wools: grays, beige/taupe plaids.

#61 - EMMA LOU'S SKY BLUE
POT LUCK METHOD

1/4 t   Silver Gray ⎫
1/4 t   Blue   ⎬ 1 CBW
                      ⎭

Use 1/4 cup.

Wools: grays - beige/taupe plaids.

#62 - MICHAEL'S DENIM BLUE
POT LUCK METHOD

1/2 t   Blue   ⎫
1/16 t   Plum   ⎬ 1 CBW
2/16 t   Gold   ⎭

Use 1/4 cup.

Wools: grays.

#63 - JACK BOY BLUE
POT LUCK METHOD

1/4 t   Sky Blue   ⎫
1/4 t   Navy Blue   ⎬ 1 CBW
1/4 t   Silver Gray ⎪
2/32 t   Jade Green   ⎭

Use 1/2 cup.

Wools: grays.

#64 – BARB'S MIDNIGHT BLUE
POT LUCK METHOD

1-1/4 t	Blue	⎫
1/2 t	Dark Brown	⎬ 1 CBW
1/4 t + 2/32 t	Dark Green	⎭

Use 2/3 cup.

Wools: grays. Makes great dark background.

#65 – EMMA LOU'S ANTIQUE BLUE
POT LUCK METHOD

1-1/4 t	Blue	⎫
3/4 t + 2/32 t	Black	⎬ 1 CBW
2/32 t	Old Gold	⎭

Use 1/2 cup.

Wools: grays. Makes great dark background.

#66 – EMMA LOU'S & BARB'S TEALY BLUE
POT LUCK METHOD

3/8 t	Blue	⎫
1/8 t	Jade Green	⎪
1/4 t	Peacock	⎬ 1 CBW
1/32 t	Taupe	⎪
1/32 t	Black	⎭

Use 1/4 cup.

Wools: grays.

#67 – WOOLLEY FOX BLUE
POT LUCK METHOD

3/8 t	Blue	⎫
1/8 t	Jade Green	⎪
1/4 t	Peacock	⎬ 1 CBW
1/32 t	Taupe	⎪
1/32 t	Black	⎪
3/32 t	Garnet	⎭

Use 1/4 cup.

Wools: beige, gray, taupe.

#68 – BUTTERMILK PAINT BLUE
POT LUCK METHOD

1/2 t	Turquoise	⎫
1/16 t	Burgundy	⎬ 1 CBW
1/16 t	Khaki Drab	⎭

Use 1/4 cup.

Wools: beige, gray, beige/taupe plaids.

#69 – HIAWATHA BLUE
POT LUCK METHOD

1/2 t	Turquoise Blue	⎫
1/16 t	Burgundy	⎬ 1 CBW
1/16 t	Khaki Drab	⎭

Use 1/4 cup.

Wools: beige, gray, beige/taupe plaids.

#70 – JOHN JOSEPH'S COAT
POT LUCK METHOD

1/8 t	Aqua	⎫
1/8 t	Turquoise Blue	⎬ 1 CBW
1/8 t	Silver Gray	⎭

Use 1/4 cup.

Wools: beige, gray, beige/taupe plaids.

#71 – ALLIE'S JADE
POT LUCK METHOD

3/4 t	Turquoise	⎫
3/8 t	Jade Green	⎬ 1 CBW
2/32 t	Egyptian Red	⎭

Use 1/4 cup.

Wools: beige, gray, beige/taupe plaids.

#72 – BARB'S MAGIC SHOW
POT LUCK METHOD

3/4 t	Turquoise	⎫
3/8 t	Jade Green	⎪
1/4 t + 2/32 t	Bright Purple	⎬ 1 CBW
3/32 t	Garnet	⎪
1/4 t	Chartreuse	⎭

Use 1/4 + 1/8 cup.

Wools: grays.

The Formulas for

ANTIQUE
LIGHTS
&
MEDIUMS

#73 – FAMILY & FRIENDS
A LA CARTE METHOD

Mix:
1/4 t	Seal Brown – 1 CBW
1/4 t	Golden Brown – 1 CBW

Use:
2 t	Seal Brown solution
2 t	Golden Brown solution

Wools: light beige, light plaids.
For light, warm background. For medium
tones, increase dye solutions.

#74 – GAYLE'S FAVORITE LIGHT
POT LUCK METHOD

3/8 t	Khaki Drab	⎫
1/16 t	Golden Brown	⎬ 1 CBW
1/16 t	Woodrose	⎭

For lighter – 3 t
For medium – 1T
For darker – 1-1/2 T in dye pot.

Wools: light beiges, light taupes,
oatmeal. Grayed Khaki-Green backgrounds.

#75 - JOAN'S "ONION SKIN" (Paul's mom)

Warm, buttery yellow

1 t	Ecru	⎫
1 t	Old Ivory	⎬ 8 CBW
1 t	Champagne	⎭

yields 8 cups of "onion skin" liquid

Method – using "Soup Pot":
Pour 2 cups of hot water in bottom of pan. Layer wool - sprinkle uniodized salt and 1 cup of "Onion Skin" liquid. Then layer wool again repeating entire process until all Onion Skin liquid is used, ending with Onion Skin liquid. Cover pot with aluminum foil, punch holes in top and let pot and wool simmer for 40-45 minutes. You can use dark, medium and light wools. Emma Lou and Barb use this method over already dyed wools.

For a great light background:

1/4 t	Ecru	⎫
1/4 t	Old Ivory	⎬ 2 CBW
1/4 t	Champagne	⎭

Over light wools, white, oatmeal, taupes.
Use 3T, 5T, 8T of dye solution.

#76 - SPRINGTIME GREEN
A LA CARTE METHOD

Mix:
1/4 t	Bronze - 1/2 CBW
1/4 t	Medium Brown - 1/2 CBW

In pot use:
4 t	Bronze
1/2 t	Medium Brown

Wools: white, beiges, tans, plaid texture.
NOTE: medium shades are lovely.

#77 - KHAKI
A LA CARTE METHOD

Mix:
1/2 t	Khaki Drab – 1 CBW	
1/2 t	Medium Brown – 1 CBW	

In pot use:
2 T	Khaki Drab
1 T	Medium Brown
or	
4 T	Khaki Drab
2 T	Medium Brown

Wools:.white and light tan, taupe, beige.

#78 - NANCY'S CASHMERE
Warm Beige
POT LUCK METHOD

2/32 t	Rust	⎫
2/32 t	Bronze	⎬ 1 CBW
1/8 t	Medium Brown	⎭

Use 5 teaspoons.

Wools: white and light tan, taupe, beige.

#79 - OLD BEIGE
POT LUCK METHOD

1/4 t	Old Gold	⎫
1/4 t	Golden Brown	⎬ 1 CBW
1/8 t	Dark Gray	⎭

Use 5 teaspoons.

Wools: white and light tan, taupe, beige.

#80 - GRAYED TAUPE
A LA CARTE METHOD

1/2 t   Seal Brown - 1 CBW

Use 3 t - 5 t

Wools: white, light gray textures or Dorr 8218
NOTE: dyed over beiges gives warmer hues.
Emma Lou uses this quite often for a
background for her "Old Saltbox with Willow
Trees" pattern.

#81 - SOFT KHAKI
A LA CARTE METHOD

Mix:
1/2 t   Medium Brown - 1 CBW
1/2 t   Khaki Drab - 1 CBW
In pot use:
2 T   Medium Brown
1 T   Khaki Drab

Wools: white, light tans, taupe, beiges -
plaids.

#82 - ABBY'S ROSE
Musty Rose
POT LUCK METHOD

1/4 t   Mulberry   ⎫
2/32 t Ecru   ⎬ 1 CBW
2/32 t Bronze Green ⎭

Use 4 or 5 teaspoons.

Wools: white, light tans, taupes, beiges,
plaids.

#83 - PRIMROSE
POT LUCK METHOD

1/4 t	Woodrose	⎫
2/32 t	Old Ivory	⎬ 1 CBW
1/32 t	Bronze	⎭

Use 6 teaspoons.

Wools: white, light beiges, tan, taupes, textures.

#84 - BARB'S PLAYTIME
Peachy–Rusty
POT LUCK METHOD

1/4 t	Mahogany	⎫
2/32 t	Rust	⎪
4/32 t	Bronze	⎬ 1 CBW
2/32 t	Mummy Brown	⎪
2/32 t	Seal Brown	⎭

Use 4 teaspoons.

Wools: white, light beiges, tan, taupes, textures.

#85 - EMMA LOU'S PUTTY (OLD)
POT LUCK METHOD

1 t	Taupe	⎫
3/32 t	Khaki Drab	⎬ 1 CBW
speck of	Black	⎭
(1/2 of 1/32 t)		

Use 4 teaspoons.

Wools: white, light beiges, tan, taupes, textures.

#86 - CHEERS TO MAGGIE
In Memory of Margaret Hunt Masters
POT LUCK METHOD

1/4 t + 1/32 t	Khaki Drab	⎫
1/8 t + 1/32 t	Woodrose	⎬ 1 CBW
2/32 t	Med. Brown	⎭

Use 5 teaspoons.

Wools: white, light beiges, taupe, tan.

This is a fun formula to play with. You can alter this in lots of ways. Below are a few suggestions:

1/8 t + 2/32 t	Khaki Drab	⎫
1/4 t	Woodrose	⎬ 1 CBW
2/32 t	Med. Brown	⎭

1/4 t	Khaki Drab	⎫
1/8 t + 1/32 t	Woodrose	⎬ 1 CBW
1/8 t	Med. Brown	⎭

If you want your colour greener, use more Khaki Drab; more rosy, add more Woodrose; or browner, use more Medium Brown. This gives you the freedom to use your imagination.

Other ideas for Antique Light and Medium Backgrounds:

Again, you can use the following formulas in their lightest and medium shades.

Remember to use less dye and lighter colour wools to help you achieve the right shade.

GREENS:

#22 - Our Old Reseda
#33 - Gerry's Moon & Star

BLUES:

#60 - Emma Lou's Smoky Blue
#61 - Emma Lou's Sky Blue
#69 - Hiawatha Blue
#70 - John Joseph's Coat

The Formulas for

ANTIQUE DARKS

#88 – HOOK BOOK BLACK
POT LUCK METHOD

t	Olive Green	⎫
/2 t	Dark Brown	⎬ 1 CBW
/4 t	Black	⎭

Use all in one pot.

Wools: Barb always dyes this over red plaids.

#89 – ANTIQUE BLACK GREEN
POT LUCK METHOD

/2 t	Black	⎫
/2 t	Khaki Drab	⎬ 1 CBW
/2 t	Dark Green	⎭

Use all in one pot.

Wools: grays – plaids, herringbones.

#90 – ANTIQUE BLACK
POT LUCK METHOD

/16 t	Plum	⎫
/4 t	Khaki Drab	⎬ 1 CBW
/4 t	Peacock	⎪
1/8 t	Black	⎭

Use all in one pot.

Wools: greens – plaids, etc.

#91 - ANTIQUE BROWN-BLACK
A LA CARTE METHOD

Mix:
1 t	Medium Brown -	1 CBW
1 t	Golden Brown -	1/2 CBW
1/2 t	Black -	1/2 CBW

In pot use for medium dark:
10 T	Medium Brown
3 T	Golden Brown
2 T	Black

In pot use for darker::
16 T	Medium Brown
4 1/2 T	Golden Brown
3 T	Black

Wools: grays.

#92 - ANTIQUE MAHOGANY
POT LUCK METHOD

1 t	Mahogany	⎫
1/2 t	Dark Brown	⎬ 1 CBW
		⎭

Use 3/4 cup in pot.

Wools: taupes and browns.

#93 - WINE IS FINE
POT LUCK METHOD

1 t	Wine	⎫
1 t	Maroon	⎬ 1 CBW
1/2 t	Bronze Green	⎭

Use all in one pot.

Wools: grays.

94 - RICH & WARM ANTIQUE DARK
OT LUCK METHOD

t	Mahogany	⎤
t	Dark Brown	⎬ 1 CBW
/2 t	Plum	⎜
/4 t	Black	⎦

se all in one pot.

Vools: grays and browns.

#95 - ANTIQUE DARK DARK
OT LUCK METHOD

-1/4 t	Dark Green	⎤
/2 t	Seal Brown	⎬ 1 CBW
/2 t	Dark Gray	⎦

se 3/4 cup.

Vools: grays and greens.

Also, for Antique Dark Backgrounds:

You can use the following formulas in their dark shades and over dark wools. There are some yummy ones here:

REDS/PURPLES:

#1B – Nancy's Naughty Red
#2A – Old Main Red
#2B – Shakespeare Red
#5 – Taco Bean Red
#6 – Nicholas Red
#12 – Emma Lou's Favorite Red
#14 – Deep Purple

GREENS:

#21 – Barb's Reseda
#23 – Juniper Blue-Green
#24 – Barb's Marvelous Myrtle
#29 – Khaki Bronze
#32 – Emma Lou's Hunter
#33 – Gerry's Moon and Star

GOLDS:

#40A – New York Bronze
#40B – Bronzy Spark
#40C – Kansas City Bronze
#41 – Big Al Gold
#42 – Our New Golden Brown

BLUES:

#64 – Barb's Midnight Blue
#65 – Emma Lou's Antique Blue
#67 – Woolley Fox Blue
#72 – Barb's Magic Show

The Formulas for

BROWNS

&

RUSTS

#97 – ROBIN'S 1909 HORSE
A LA CARTE METHOD

Mix:

1/2 t	Medium Brown	– 1 CBW
1/2 t	Golden Brown	– 1 CBW
1/2 t	Rust	– 1 CBW
1/2 t	Black	– 1 CBW

In pot use:

10 T	Medium Brown
2 T	Golden Brown
1 T	Rust
1 T	Black

Wools: blue–grays, blue herringbones and grays.

#98 – MOOSE ON THE LOOSE BROWN
POT LUCK METHOD

1/2 t	Spice Brown	
1/4 t	Medium Brown	} 1 CBW
3/32 t	Olive Green	
2/32 t	Black	

Use 1/4 cup for lighter tones, and 1/2 cup for darker tones.

Wools: beige, browns, taupes and tan.

#99 – KATHY'S FOX
POT LUCK METHOD

1/2 t	Mummy Brown	
1/4 t	Rust	} 1 CBW
1/32 t	Copenhagen Blue	

Use 1/2 cup for lighter tones.
Use 3/4 cup for darker tones.

Wools: tan, beige, browns and great over greens.

#100 – TERRA COTTA CLAY
A LA CARTE METHOD

Mix:

1/2 t	Terra Cotta – 1 CBW
1/2 t	Rust – 1 CBW
1/2 t	Medium Brown – 1 CBW

Use in pot:

6 T	Terra Cotta
4 T	Rust
8 T	Medium Brown

Wools: tan, beige and brown.

#101 – LAUREL MOUNTAIN POSY
POT LUCK METHOD

1/4 t	Rust	⎫
1/4 t	Mahogany	⎬ 1 CBW
1/4 t	Egyptian Red	⎭

Use 1/8 cup.

Wools: tan, beige, and brown.

#102 – OLD APRICOT
POT LUCK METHOD

1/2 t	Rust	⎫
1/4 t	Mahogany	⎪
2/32 t	Egyptian Red	⎬ 1 CBW
4/32 t	Medium Brown	⎪
3/32 t	Olive Green	⎭

Use 1/8 cup.

Wools: tans, taupes and beiges.

#103 – EMMA LOU'S PUMPKIN PATCH

POT LUCK METHOD

1/2 t	Rust	⎫
1/32 t	Old Gold	⎜
3/32 t	Gold	⎬ 1 CBW
2/32 t	Golden Brown	⎜
1/32 t	Orange	⎭

Use all

Wools: tans, browns, beiges, fun plaids.

The Formulas for

UNUSUAL COLOURS FOR PRIMITIVE RUGS

#110 – TURQUOISE SPARK
POT LUCK METHOD

1 1/4 t	Turquoise Green	⎫
1/32 t	Maroon	⎬ 1 CBW
2/32 t	Black	⎭

Use 1/2 cub

Wools: tans, beiges, light brown.

#111 – BARB'S WILD BERRY
POT LUCK METHOD

1/2 t	Cardinal	⎫
2/32 t	Bright Purple	⎬ 1 CBW
2/32 t	Hunter Green	⎭

Use 1/2 cup.

Wools: tan, beige, and light brown.

#112 – KELLY'S PERIWINKLE
POT LUCK METHOD

1/4 t	Copenhagen Blue	⎫
3/32 t	Bright Purple	⎬ 1 CBW
		⎭

Use 2 T – light Use 6 T – darker

Wools: light to medium grays.

#113 – ROOSTER LADY'S PURPLE
POT LUCK METHOD

1/2 t	Plum	⎫
2/32 t	Chartruese	⎬ 1 CBW
1/4 t	Maroon	⎪
1/4 t	Copenhagen Blue	⎭

For lighter shade use 1 T
For darker shade use 6 T

Wools: light to medium grays.

#114 – OLD WILD ROSE
POT LUCK METHOD

1/2 t	Old Rose	⎫
1/8 t	Wild Rose	⎬ 1 CBW
2/32 t	Bronze Green	⎭

Use 2 T

Wools: light to mid grays, light tans & taupe beiges (over the tans it gives a rosier shade).

#115 – BARB'S BUTTERED SQUASH
POT LUCK METHOD

1 t	Apricot	⎫
3/32 t	Ecru	⎬ 1 CBW
		⎭

Use 3 T

Wools: very light tans and beiges.

#116 – MORE SQUASH
POT LUCK METHOD

1/2 t	Golden Brown	⎫
2/32 t	Orange	⎬ 1 CBW
2/32 t	Medium Brown	⎭

Use 1/2 cup.

Wools: tans, taupes, beiges, and browns.

We worked specifically to try to recreate some of the unusual colours found in the antique primitive rugs.

These can be used for spark, poison, or an important part of your rug.

We also suggest the use of the following formulas for this.

> #15 – Molly's Purple Garnet
> #16 – Mulberry Patch
> #40 – New York Bronze
> #47 – California Gold
> #66 – Emma Lou & Barb's Tealy Blue
> #72 – Barb's Magic Show

This section is to encourage you to continue a movement of a sense of fun and freedom in your primitive rugs.

FLESH (not shown)

Mix 1/2 t Rust – 1 CBW

Use 3 pans:

First pan	1/4 t rust dye solution
Second pan	1/2 t rust dye solution
Third pan	3/4 t rust dye solution

Wools: use over natural wools.

Take a piece of the "darker" rust wool and dye just a "wash" of Egyptian Red (mixed 1/2 t to 1 CBW) _very_ lightly over some of it. This will be lovely cheeks and mouth for a girl. Take another piece of the "darker" rust wool and dye just a "wash" of Mahogany (mixed 1/2 t to 1 CBW) _very_ lightly over some of it. This will be a great colour for cheeks and nose for a boy. Barb sometimes does a "wash" of blue (mixed 1/2 t to 1 CBW) over all to age and soften the "flesh."

PEACHY FLESH (not shown)
POT LUCK METHOD

1/2 t	Rust	⎫
1/8 t	Terra Cotta	⎬ 1 CBW
1/32 t	American Beauty	⎭

Use 3 pans:
First pan - 1/8 t dye solution
Second pan - 1/4 t dye solution
Third pan - 3/8 t dye solution

Wools: use over natural or very light beiges.

PEASE PORRIDGE POT (not shown)

Unopened packets of dry dye can be stored a long time. After mixing the dye in boiling water, it is only useable for a few weeks. After that, sometimes the colour changes.

So, you've been dyeing up lots of colours and you have a little bit of this and a little bit of that, or maybe a lot of this and that! What do you do with your left-over dyes?

Both Emma Lou and Barb pour it all into a large. empty vinegar bottle and, when we have enough (different for everyone), we use it to over-dye ugly and boring wools for great deep backgrounds.

In the pot, add water, 1 tablespoon of salt, and start with 3/4 cup of **Pease Porridge Pot.** Add more as needed to get a nice, deep background - maybe up to 2 1/2 cups of **Pease Porridge Pot.** Bring to a simmer, add your wools, stir a few times, and then slow simmer for about 2 hours before you add your vinegar. If you need more dye, add it before you put in the vinegar.

PEASE PORRIDGE POT continued

This is a great fun way to get unusual background colours and avoid storing leftover dyes for too long on your shelf.

Part of the fun of **Pease Porridge Pot** is the surprise of the colour of the antique dark background you will be dyeing. Using either a white enamel spoon or white paper towels, test the **Pease Porridge Pot** dye to see which colour shows the strongest. If the colour has a tendency towards blue, Barb dyes this over gray, blue, black and purple plaids, checks, tweed, etc. If brown is the strongest colour, then she uses green, red and orange textures. So, if red is strongesr, use **Pease Porridge Pot** over brown, green, and orange textures. Finally, if **Pease Porridge Pot** shows a tendency towards black, use over red, green, fushia, purple and gray textures.

When you dye these "darks" over the different plaids, wonderful colourations "pop" up as you hook, giving you a subtle but very interesting background.

This is a fun way to dye and create a one-time "colour story." So, be sure to save up enough dye in your vinegar jug to dye plenty of wool background. This is one time you don't want to be caught short!!

A NOTE ABOUT THE
COLOUR SWATCHES

No printing process using ink on flat paper can hope to reproduce the richness of colour and depth of texture of the original swatches produced by Emma Lou and Barb while creating this book. The colour swatches on the following pages are presented as guides, your specific results may vary.

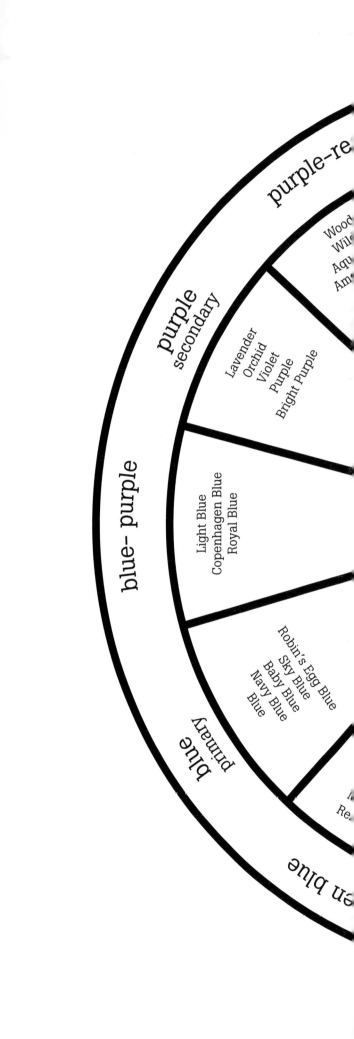

purple-re

purple
secondary

blue–purple

blue
primary

en blue

Wood
Wile
Aqu
Am

Lavender
Orchid
Violet
Purple
Bright Purple

Light Blue
Copenhagen Blue
Royal Blue

Robin's Egg Blue
Sky Blue
Baby Blue
Navy Blue
Blue

Re

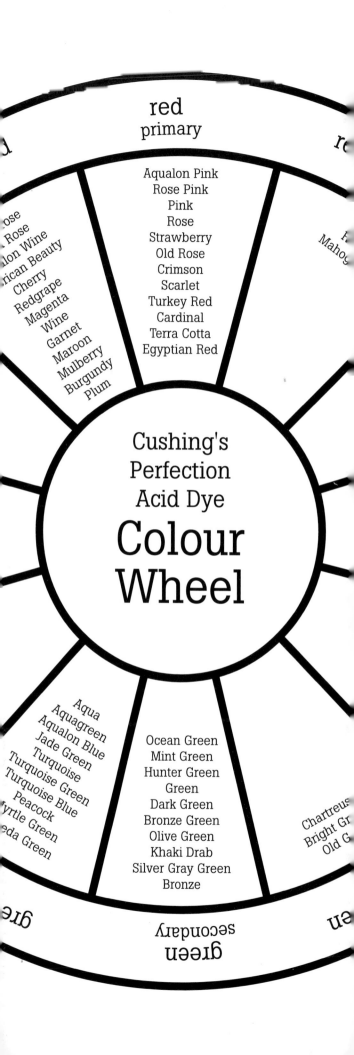

red
primary

Aqualon Pink
Rose Pink
Pink
Rose
Strawberry
Old Rose
Crimson
Scarlet
Turkey Red
Cardinal
Terra Cotta
Egyptian Red

...ose
...Rose
...lon Wine
...rican Beauty
Cherry
Redgrape
Magenta
Wine
Garnet
Maroon
Mulberry
Burgundy
Plum

Mahog...

Cushing's
Perfection
Acid Dye
Colour
Wheel

Aqua
Aquagreen
Aqualon Blue
Jade Green
Turquoise
Turquoise Green
Turquoise Blue
Peacock
...yrtle Green
...eda Green

Ocean Green
Mint Green
Hunter Green
Green
Dark Green
Bronze Green
Olive Green
Khaki Drab
Silver Gray Green
Bronze

Chartreus...
Bright Gr...
Old G...

gre...
green
secondary
...en

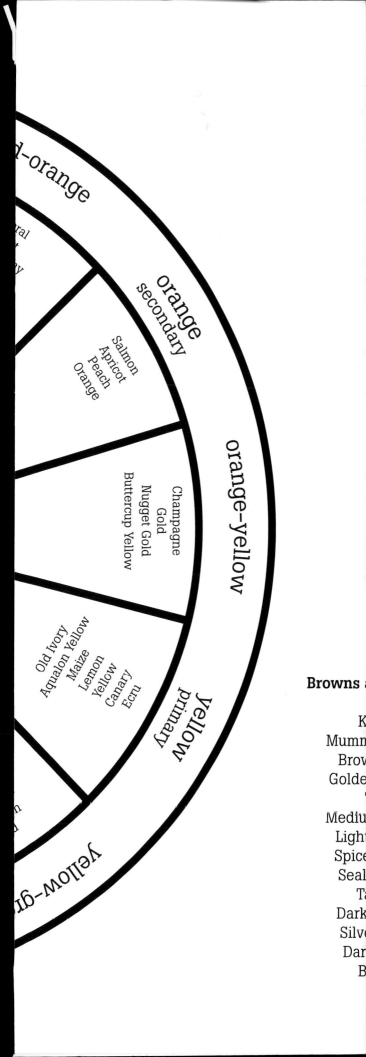

and Browns

haki
ny Brown
vn Rust
n Brown
Tan
m Brown
 Brown
e Brown
 Brown
aupe
 Brown
er Gray
k Gray
lack

Browns and Rusts (#99 – #103)
Unusual Colours for Primitive Rugs

#99 – Kathy's Fox
p. 69

#100 – Terra Cotta Clay
p. 70

#101 – Laurel Mountain
Posy p. 70

#102– Old Apricot
p. 70

#103 – Emma Lou's
Pumpkin Patch p. 71

#110 – Turquoise Spark
p. 75

#111 – Barb's Wild
Berry p. 75

#112 – Kelly's
Periwinkle p. 75

#113 – Rooster Lady's
Purple p. 75

#114 – Old Wild Rose
p. 76

#115 – Barb's Buttered
Squash p. 76

#116 – More Squash
p. 76

Antique Darks
Browns and Rusts (#97 & #98)

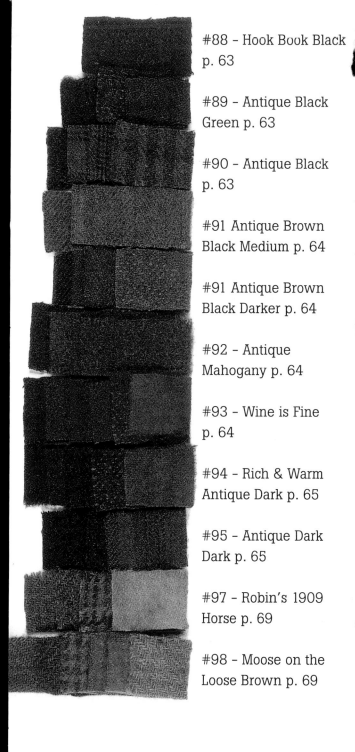

#88 – Hook Book Black
p. 63

#89 – Antique Black
Green p. 63

#90 – Antique Black
p. 63

#91 Antique Brown
Black Medium p. 64

#91 Antique Brown
Black Darker p. 64

#92 – Antique
Mahogany p. 64

#93 – Wine is Fine
p. 64

#94 – Rich & Warm
Antique Dark p. 65

#95 – Antique Dark
Dark p. 65

#97 – Robin's 1909
Horse p. 69

#98 – Moose on the
Loose Brown p. 69

Antique Lights and Mediums

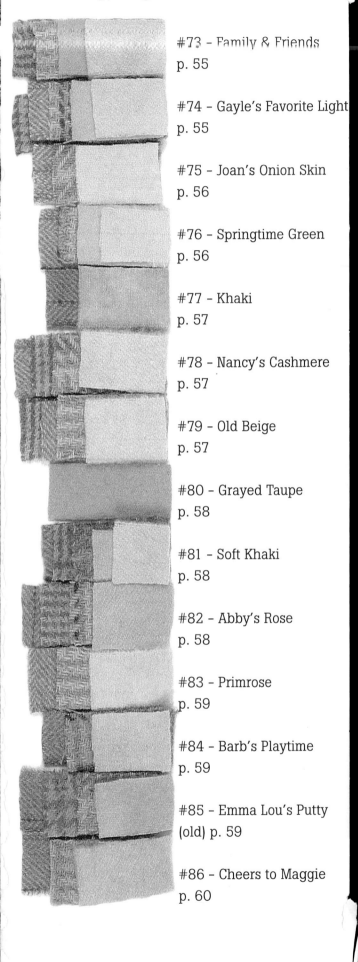

Blues